XTREME PETS
DOGS

BY S.L. HAMILTON

www.abdopublishing.com

Published by ABDO Publishing Company, PO Box 398166, Minneapolis, MN 55439.

Printed in the United States of America, North Mankato, Minnesota.
042013
012014

PRINTED ON RECYCLED PAPER

Editor: John Hamilton
Graphic Design: Sue Hamilton
Cover Design: Sue Hamilton
Cover Photo: AP
Interior Photos: Alamy-pg 7 (Irish wolfhound) ; AP-pgs 4-5, 6, 24 (inset); Corbis-pgs 13 (top left), 19 (top), 22, 23 (top), 26 (inset) & 27 (inset); DreamsTime-pgs 8, 9, 21 (bottom), 23 (bottom), 24 & 30-31; Getty-pgs 13 (bottom), 28 & 29 (top); Glow Images-pgs 12, 13 (top right), 16, 17 (top), 20, 21 (top), 25 & 29 (bottom); iStock-pgs 15 & 20 (inset); Thinkstock-pgs 1, 2-3, 10, 11, 12 (inset), 14, 17 (bottom left & right), 18, 19 (bottom), 26, 27 & 32.

ABDO Booklinks
Web sites about Xtreme Pets are featured on our Book Links pages. These links are routinely monitored and updated to provide the most current information available.
Web site: www.abdopublishing.com

Library of Congress Control Number: 2013931670

Cataloging-in-Publication Data

Hamilton, Sue.
 Dogs / Sue Hamilton.
   p. cm. -- (Xtreme pets)
ISBN 978-1-61783-972-6
1. Dogs--Juvenile literature. 2. Pets--Juvenile literature.   I. Title.
636.7--dc23

2013931670

CONTENTS

Xtreme Pets: Dogs 4

Tallest Dogs 6

Heaviest Dogs 8

Smallest Dogs 10

Smartest Dogs 12

Hairiest Dogs 16

Hairless Dogs 18

Fastest Dogs 20

Best Swimmers 22

Best Noses and Longest Ears 24

Longest-Lived Dogs 28

Glossary 30

Index 32

Today's many dog breeds likely began from wolves thousands of years ago. Today, the American Kennel Club lists 157 dog breeds. More than 5,000 varieties of these dog breeds run, jump, bark, drool, shake, swim, and wag their way into our hearts. Some of these dogs have grown into unusual and amazing four-footed friends.

XTREME FACT –
People who love dogs are
known as "caninophiles."

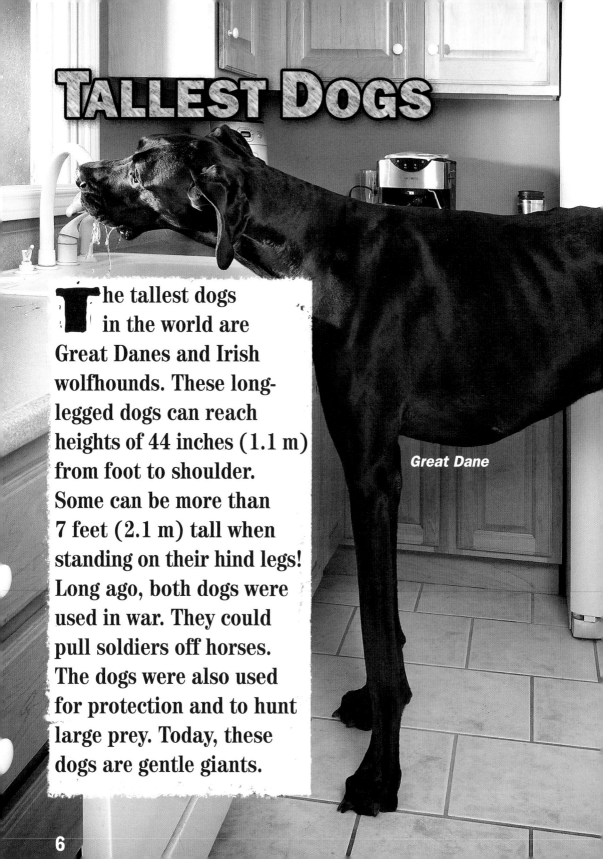

TALLEST DOGS

The tallest dogs in the world are Great Danes and Irish wolfhounds. These long-legged dogs can reach heights of 44 inches (1.1 m) from foot to shoulder. Some can be more than 7 feet (2.1 m) tall when standing on their hind legs! Long ago, both dogs were used in war. They could pull soldiers off horses. The dogs were also used for protection and to hunt large prey. Today, these dogs are gentle giants.

Great Dane

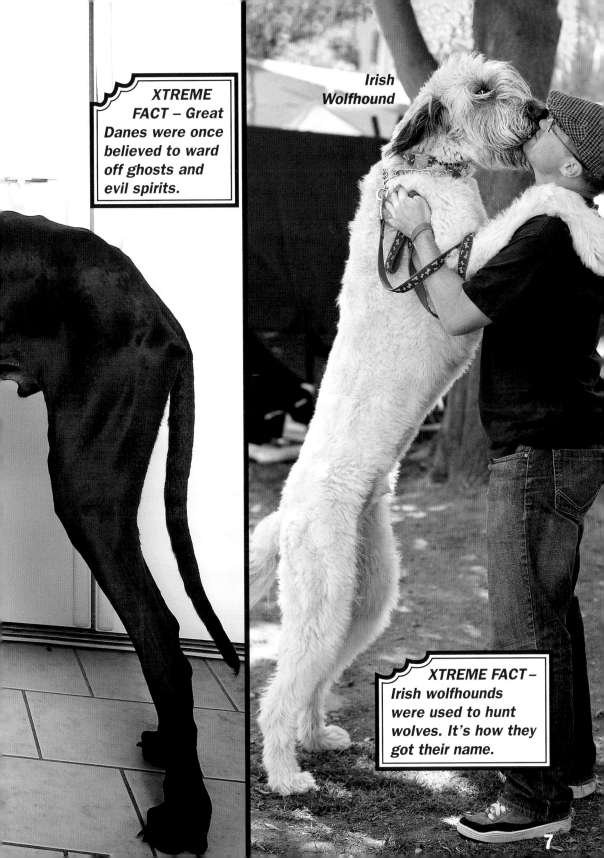

XTREME FACT – Great Danes were once believed to ward off ghosts and evil spirits.

Irish Wolfhound

XTREME FACT – Irish wolfhounds were used to hunt wolves. It's how they got their name.

HEAVIEST DOGS

Mastiffs and Saint Bernards are the heaviest pet dogs. They can weigh up to 200 pounds (91 kg). English mastiffs are 25-36 inches (64-91 cm) from foot to shoulder.

Mastiff

XTREME FACT – The heaviest dog was an English mastiff named Zorba at 343 pounds (156 kg).

Saint Bernards have big bones and muscles, and heavy fluffy coats. Monks in Switzerland used the gentle Saint Bernards to lead them up snowy mountain passes and to rescue people. Saint Bernards are said to be able to find people buried in as deep as 14 feet (4.3 m) of snow.

Saint Bernard

XTREME FACT – *Pairs of Saint Bernards worked as rescue teams in the Swiss Alps. One dog would lay down to keep the injured person warm, while the other went for help.*

SMALLEST DOGS

Chihuahuas, Japanese Chin, and Yorkshire terriers are the smallest dog breeds.

Chihuahuas came from Mexico. They weigh 4-6 pounds (2-3 kg) and are 6-9 inches (15-23 cm) tall. Although they are tiny, they have large brains.

Chihuahua

Great Dane

Yorkshire terriers weigh about 5-7 pounds (2-3 kg) and are 9 inches (23 cm) tall from foot to shoulder. Yorkies were bred to chase rats out of factories in northern England. They are smart and fast.

Yorkshire Terrier

Japanese Chins weigh 4-7 pounds (2-3 kg) and are 8-11 inches (20-28 cm) tall. These dogs, which were believed to originate in China (not Japan), were bred to be companions to Japanese royalty. They are also known as Japanese spaniels.

Japanese Chin

SMARTEST DOGS

Three of the smartest dogs are border collies, poodles, and German shepherds. These dogs obey a command the first time it's given 95 percent of the time or better.

Border Collie

Border collies were bred to herd sheep, either by command or on their own. Border collies have an intense stare called "the eye." They use this extreme focus to intimidate.

Poodle

Poodles are a very smart breed. Besides being excellent pets, they are hunting dogs, entertainers, and service dogs.

Intelligent, strong, and loyal, German shepherds are one of the most popular dogs. They also work in the military and law enforcement. German shepherds follow commands. They will attack an enemy, and even more importantly, stop an attack as instructed.

German Shepherd

German shepherds are excellent search and rescue dogs. They are tireless in searching for someone lost or hurt.

XTREME FACT – One of the most famous German shepherds was 1920s star Rin Tin Tin. The smart dog's successful movies helped save Warner Brothers Studios from financial ruin.

HAIRIEST DOGS

The hairiest dog breed is the komondor. Its coat alone can weigh 15 pounds (7 kg) and have more than 2,000 cords. The thick coat protects the herding dog from cold weather. It also allows the komondor to blend into a flock of sheep so it can sneak up on an attacking wolf or bear.

Komondor

Hungarian Puli

Other very hairy pets include the Hungarian puli (which looks like a komondor but is about a quarter of its size), the Afghan hound, and the Old English sheepdog. These dogs are all herding dogs.

Afghan Hound

Old English Sheepdog

17

HAIRLESS DOGS

A few breeds of dogs have little or no hair or fur. These include the Chinese crested, the Peruvian Inca Orchid, and the Mexican Xoloitzcuintli.

Chinese Crested

Chinese crested dogs were bred to catch rats on ships. Their lack of hair meant that fleas from the rats couldn't hide on them and then infest the sailors.

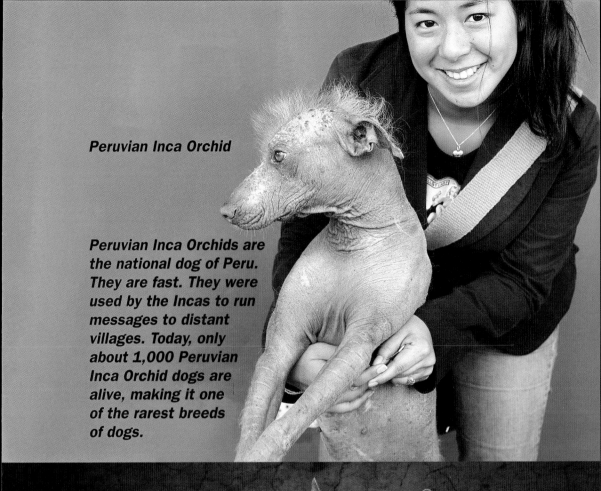

Peruvian Inca Orchid

Peruvian Inca Orchids are the national dog of Peru. They are fast. They were used by the Incas to run messages to distant villages. Today, only about 1,000 Peruvian Inca Orchid dogs are alive, making it one of the rarest breeds of dogs.

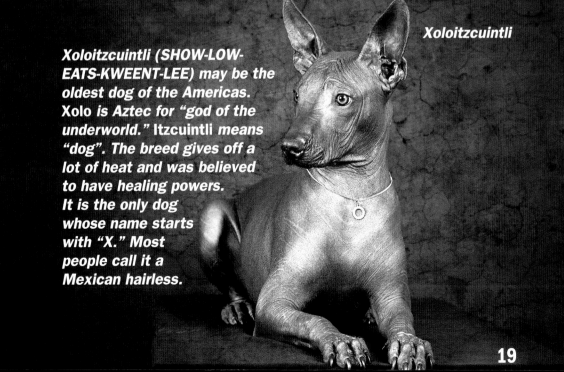

Xoloitzcuintli

Xoloitzcuintli (SHOW-LOW-EATS-KWEENT-LEE) may be the oldest dog of the Americas. Xolo *is Aztec for "god of the underworld."* Itzcuintli *means "dog".* The breed gives off a lot of heat and was believed to have healing powers. It is the only dog whose name starts with "X." Most people call it a Mexican hairless.

FASTEST DOGS

The fastest dogs are greyhounds. Greyhounds have narrow aerodynamic bodies and long muscular legs. They can reach speeds up to 45 miles per hour (72 kph). That's more than one and a half times as fast as the fastest human sprinter!

Greyhound

XTREME FACT – Greyhounds may be fast, but they really like to relax and lay around. They are nicknamed "the 40-miles-per-hour-couch potato."

Salukis are a close second to greyhounds. They have been clocked at 43 mph (69 kph).

Saluki

Whippets are a smaller cousin to the greyhound. They gained their name because they are "fast as a whip." They may run up to 36 mph (58 kph).

Whippet

BEST SWIMMERS

Many dogs enjoy the water, but Newfoundland dogs, Labrador retrievers, and Portuguese water dogs are made to be wet pets. They have heavy or oily coats that protect them from cold water. They also have webbed feet, strong leg muscles, and tails that help move them through the water.

Newfoundland Dog

Many distressed swimmers have been rescued by heroic 150-pound (68-kg) Newfoundland dogs. Big leg muscles and webbed feet let these strong dogs power through waves.

Labrador retrievers were bred to be half the size of Newfoundland dogs. Strong swimmers and smart, Labs became hunting companions. They have been North America's most popular dog breed for many years.

Labrador Retriever

Portuguese Water Dog

Portuguese water dogs are excellent swimmers. They were once used by the Spanish Armada to carry messages between ships.

BEST NOSES AND LONGEST EARS

I t's no coincidence that dogs with the best noses are also the ones with the longest ears. Bloodhounds, coonhounds, basset hounds, and beagles all use their long ears to stir up scents and direct them to their super-sensitive noses.

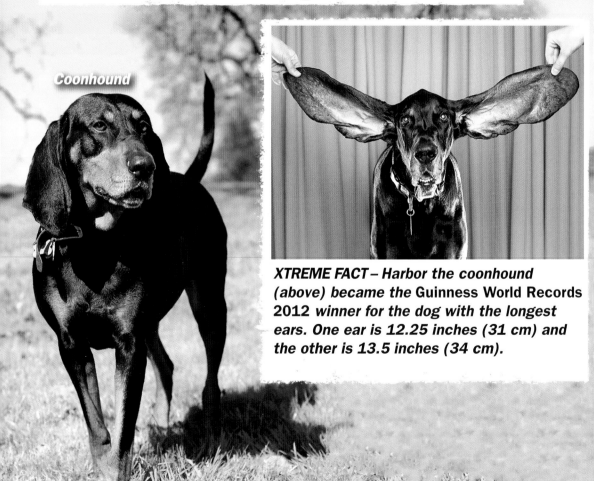

Coonhound

XTREME FACT – *Harbor the coonhound (above) became the* Guinness World Records 2012 *winner for the dog with the longest ears. One ear is 12.25 inches (31 cm) and the other is 13.5 inches (34 cm).*

Bloodhound

Bloodhounds are good at focusing on a single scent and tracking it. They can track over land and over water. Police use bloodhounds to follow trails more than two days old. Courts accept bloodhound evidence. While bloodhounds will track with extreme focus, they are not known to bite. They "bay" when they find what they have been trailing.

XTREME FACT – Bloodhounds have noses with four <u>billion</u> scent receptors. Humans only have about five million.

Basset hounds use their long ears to sweep scents up to their sensitive noses. They originally accompanied hunters on foot. Their short legs allowed them to find and flush out rabbits and other small game on the ground. Today basset hounds still have a keen sense of smell, but they are known more for their gentle disposition and soulful eyes.

Basset Hound

One of the smallest scenthounds, the long-eared beagle was originally bred to hunt rabbits. Beagles are popular as pets and as workers. Their charming face and friendly nature have made them useful at airports, where their sensitive noses are used to search luggage for illegal food, drugs, and weapons.

Beagle

LONGEST-LIVED DOGS

Small dogs such as miniature dachshunds, toy poodles, and Lhasa apsos have been found to live the longest. These dogs live an average of 12-15 years. However, with proper exercise, nutrition, and love, these pets may live up to 20 years.

Miniature Dachshund

Toy Poodle

Lhasa Apso

29

GLOSSARY

AMERICAN KENNEL CLUB (AKC)
An organization established in 1884 in the United States that determines what is an official purebred dog breed. It determines what color(s), shape, size, and physical characteristics are acceptable for each breed.

AERODYNAMIC
Something that has a shape that reduces the drag, or resistance, of air moving across its surface. Greyhounds are dogs with aerodynamic shapes. They can go faster because they don't have to push as hard to get through the air.

BREED
An animal, such as a dog or cat, with specific physical features that give it a distinct appearance from other similar animals.

CORD
Dog fur, such as on a komondor, where the undercoat and outer coat are shaped into tassel-like twists of fur that resemble dreadlocks.

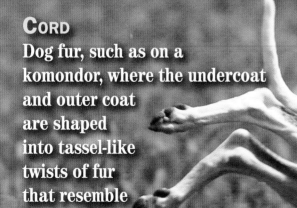

Herding Dogs
Dogs who are bred to herd or protect animals such as sheep or geese. Border collies and Old English sheepdogs are famous for their herding abilities.

Intimidate
To scare someone or something enough to make them do what is wanted. Border collies use an intense stare called "the eye" to intimidate sheep when herding.

Scent Receptors
The part of the body that allows people and animals to smell and distinguish odors. A dog's nose has far more scent receptors than a human's nose.

Scenthounds
Breeds of dogs who have noses with the best sense of smell. These include bloodhounds, coonhounds, basset hounds, and beagles. These dogs are often used as hunting companions or by police or other officials to find illegal substances or products.

INDEX

A
Afghan hound 17
American Kennel Club 4
Americas 19
Aztec 19

B
basset hound 24, 26
beagle 24, 27
bloodhound 24, 25
border collie 12

C
caninophiles 5
Chihuahua 10
China 11
Chinese crested 18
coonhound 24

D
dachshund 28

E
England 11, 13
English mastiff 8

G
German shepherd 12, 14, 15
Great Dane 6, 7
greyhound 20, 21
Guinness World Records 2012 24

H
Harbor (coonhound) 24
herding dog 16, 17
Hungarian puli 17

I
Inca 19
Irish wolfhound 6, 7

J
Japan 11
Japanese Chin 10, 11
Japanese spaniel 11

K
komondor 16, 17

L
Lab (*see* Labrador retriever)
Labrador retriever 22, 23
Lhasa apso 28, 29

M
mastiff 8
Mexican hairless 19
Mexico 10
miniature dachshund 28

N
Newfoundland dogs 22, 23
North America 23

O
Old English sheepdog 17

P
Peru 19
Peruvian Inca Orchid 18, 19
poodle 12, 13, 28, 29
Portuguese water dog 22, 23

R
Rin Tin Tin 15

S
Saint Bernard 8, 9
saluki 21
scent receptors 25
scenthound 27
Spanish Armada 23
Swiss Alps 9
Switzerland 9

T
toy poodle 28, 29

W
Warner Brothers Studios 15
whippet 21

X
Xolo (*see* Xoloitzcuintli)
Xoloitzcuintli 18, 19

Y
Yorkie (*see* Yorkshire terrier)
Yorkshire terrier 10, 11

Z
Zorba (English mastiff) 8